MW01137961

Practice Notes

This Journal Belongs To:

____

Name

____

Date

Don't miss the GOALS section at the end of this journal, starting on page 71.

Find more journals at

www.sweetharmonypress.com

Practice Notes

Practice Date	Place	Coach
Skills Practiced	Things to Remember	

Practice Date	Place	Coach
Skills Practiced	Things to Remember	

Practice Notes

Practice Date	Place	Coach
Skills Practiced	**Things to Remember**	

Practice Date	Place	Coach
Skills Practiced	**Things to Remember**	

Practice Notes

Practice Date	Place	Coach
Skills Practiced	Things to Remember	

Practice Date	Place	Coach
Skills Practiced	Things to Remember	

Practice Notes

Practice Date	Place	Coach
Skills Practiced	Things to Remember	

Practice Date	Place	Coach
Skills Practiced	Things to Remember	

Practice Notes

Practice Date	Place	Coach
Skills Practiced	Things to Remember	

Practice Date	Place	Coach
Skills Practiced	Things to Remember	

Practice Notes

Practice Date	Place	Coach
Skills Practiced	Things to Remember	

Practice Date	Place	Coach
Skills Practiced	Things to Remember	

Practice Notes

Practice Date	Place	Coach
Skills Practiced	Things to Remember	

Practice Date	Place	Coach
Skills Practiced	Things to Remember	

Practice Notes

Practice Date	Place	Coach
Skills Practiced	Things to Remember	

Practice Date	Place	Coach
Skills Practiced	Things to Remember	

Practice Notes

Practice Date	Place	Coach
Skills Practiced	Things to Remember	

Practice Date	Place	Coach
Skills Practiced	Things to Remember	

Practice Notes

Practice Date	Place	Coach
Skills Practiced	**Things to Remember**	

Practice Date	Place	Coach
Skills Practiced	**Things to Remember**	

Practice Notes

Practice Date	Place	Coach
Skills Practiced	Things to Remember	

Practice Date	Place	Coach
Skills Practiced	Things to Remember	

Practice Notes

Practice Date	Place	Coach
Skills Practiced	Things to Remember	

Practice Date	Place	Coach
Skills Practiced	Things to Remember	

Practice Notes

Practice Date	Place	Coach
Skills Practiced	Things to Remember	

Practice Date	Place	Coach
Skills Practiced	Things to Remember	

Practice Notes

Practice Date	Place	Coach
Skills Practiced	Things to Remember	

Practice Date	Place	Coach
Skills Practiced	Things to Remember	

Practice Notes

Practice Date	Place	Coach
Skills Practiced	Things to Remember	

Practice Date	Place	Coach
Skills Practiced	Things to Remember	

Practice Notes

Practice Date	Place	Coach
Skills Practiced	**Things to Remember**	

Practice Date	Place	Coach
Skills Practiced	**Things to Remember**	

Practice Notes

Practice Date	Place	Coach
Skills Practiced	Things to Remember	

Practice Date	Place	Coach
Skills Practiced	Things to Remember	

Practice Notes

Practice Date	Place	Coach
Skills Practiced	**Things to Remember**	

Practice Date	Place	Coach
Skills Practiced	**Things to Remember**	

Practice Notes

Practice Date	Place	Coach
Skills Practiced	Things to Remember	

Practice Date	Place	Coach
Skills Practiced	Things to Remember	

Practice Notes

Practice Date	Place	Coach
Skills Practiced	Things to Remember	

Practice Date	Place	Coach
Skills Practiced	Things to Remember	

Practice Notes

Practice Date	Place	Coach
Skills Practiced	Things to Remember	

Practice Date	Place	Coach
Skills Practiced	Things to Remember	

Practice Notes

Practice Date	Place	Coach
Skills Practiced	Things to Remember	

Practice Date	Place	Coach
Skills Practiced	Things to Remember	

Practice Notes

Practice Date	Place	Coach
Skills Practiced	Things to Remember	

Practice Date	Place	Coach
Skills Practiced	Things to Remember	

Practice Notes

Practice Date	Place	Coach
Skills Practiced	Things to Remember	

Practice Date	Place	Coach
Skills Practiced	Things to Remember	

Practice Notes

Practice Date	Place	Coach
Skills Practiced	Things to Remember	

Practice Date	Place	Coach
Skills Practiced	Things to Remember	

Practice Notes

Practice Date	Place	Coach
Skills Practiced	Things to Remember	

Practice Date	Place	Coach
Skills Practiced	Things to Remember	

Practice Notes

Practice Date	Place	Coach
Skills Practiced	Things to Remember	

Practice Date	Place	Coach
Skills Practiced	Things to Remember	

Practice Notes

Practice Date	Place	Coach
Skills Practiced	**Things to Remember**	

Practice Date	Place	Coach
Skills Practiced	**Things to Remember**	

Practice Notes

Practice Date	Place	Coach
Skills Practiced	Things to Remember	

Practice Date	Place	Coach
Skills Practiced	Things to Remember	

Practice Notes

Practice Date	Place	Coach
Skills Practiced	**Things to Remember**	

Practice Date	Place	Coach
Skills Practiced	**Things to Remember**	

Practice Notes

Practice Date	Place	Coach
Skills Practiced	Things to Remember	

Practice Date	Place	Coach
Skills Practiced	Things to Remember	

Practice Notes

Practice Date	Place	Coach
Skills Practiced	Things to Remember	

Practice Date	Place	Coach
Skills Practiced	Things to Remember	

Practice Notes

Practice Date	Place	Coach
Skills Practiced	Things to Remember	

Practice Date	Place	Coach
Skills Practiced	Things to Remember	

Practice Notes

Practice Date	Place	Coach
Skills Practiced	Things to Remember	

Practice Date	Place	Coach
Skills Practiced	Things to Remember	

Practice Notes

Practice Date	Place	Coach
Skills Practiced	Things to Remember	

Practice Date	Place	Coach
Skills Practiced	Things to Remember	

Practice Notes

Practice Date	Place	Coach
Skills Practiced	Things to Remember	

Practice Date	Place	Coach
Skills Practiced	Things to Remember	

Practice Notes

Practice Date	Place	Coach
Skills Practiced	**Things to Remember**	

Practice Date	Place	Coach
Skills Practiced	**Things to Remember**	

Practice Notes

Practice Date	Place	Coach
Skills Practiced	**Things to Remember**	

Practice Date	Place	Coach
Skills Practiced	**Things to Remember**	

Practice Notes

Practice Date	Place	Coach
Skills Practiced	Things to Remember	

Practice Date	Place	Coach
Skills Practiced	Things to Remember	

Practice Notes

Practice Date	Place	Coach
Skills Practiced	Things to Remember	

Practice Date	Place	Coach
Skills Practiced	Things to Remember	

Practice Notes

Practice Date	Place	Coach
Skills Practiced	Things to Remember	

Practice Date	Place	Coach
Skills Practiced	Things to Remember	

Practice Notes

Practice Date	Place	Coach
Skills Practiced	Things to Remember	

Practice Date	Place	Coach
Skills Practiced	Things to Remember	

Practice Notes

Practice Date	Place	Coach
Skills Practiced	Things to Remember	

Practice Date	Place	Coach
Skills Practiced	Things to Remember	

Practice Notes

Practice Date	Place	Coach
Skills Practiced	Things to Remember	

Practice Date	Place	Coach
Skills Practiced	Things to Remember	

Practice Notes

Practice Date	Place	Coach
Skills Practiced	Things to Remember	

Practice Date	Place	Coach
Skills Practiced	Things to Remember	

Practice Notes

Practice Date	Place	Coach
Skills Practiced	Things to Remember	

Practice Date	Place	Coach
Skills Practiced	Things to Remember	

Practice Notes

Practice Date	Place	Coach
Skills Practiced	**Things to Remember**	

Practice Date	Place	Coach
Skills Practiced	**Things to Remember**	

Practice Notes

Practice Date	Place	Coach
Skills Practiced	**Things to Remember**	

Practice Date	Place	Coach
Skills Practiced	**Things to Remember**	

Practice Notes

Practice Date	Place	Coach
Skills Practiced	**Things to Remember**	

Practice Date	Place	Coach
Skills Practiced	**Things to Remember**	

Practice Notes

Practice Date	Place	Coach
Skills Practiced	Things to Remember	

Practice Date	Place	Coach
Skills Practiced	Things to Remember	

Practice Notes

Practice Date	Place	Coach
Skills Practiced	**Things to Remember**	

Practice Date	Place	Coach
Skills Practiced	**Things to Remember**	

Practice Notes

Practice Date	Place	Coach
Skills Practiced	**Things to Remember**	

Practice Date	Place	Coach
Skills Practiced	**Things to Remember**	

Practice Notes

Practice Date	Place	Coach
Skills Practiced	Things to Remember	

Practice Date	Place	Coach
Skills Practiced	Things to Remember	

Practice Notes

Practice Date	Place	Coach
Skills Practiced	**Things to Remember**	

Practice Date	Place	Coach
Skills Practiced	**Things to Remember**	

Practice Notes

Practice Date	Place	Coach
Skills Practiced	Things to Remember	

Practice Date	Place	Coach
Skills Practiced	Things to Remember	

Practice Notes

Practice Date	Place	Coach
Skills Practiced	**Things to Remember**	

Practice Date	Place	Coach
Skills Practiced	**Things to Remember**	

Practice Notes

Practice Date	Place	Coach
Skills Practiced	**Things to Remember**	

Practice Date	Place	Coach
Skills Practiced	**Things to Remember**	

Practice Notes

Practice Date	Place	Coach
Skills Practiced	**Things to Remember**	

Practice Date	Place	Coach
Skills Practiced	**Things to Remember**	

Practice Notes

Practice Date	Place	Coach
Skills Practiced	Things to Remember	

Practice Date	Place	Coach
Skills Practiced	Things to Remember	

Practice Notes

Practice Date	Place	Coach
Skills Practiced	**Things to Remember**	

Practice Date	Place	Coach
Skills Practiced	**Things to Remember**	

Practice Notes

Practice Date	Place	Coach
Skills Practiced	Things to Remember	

Practice Date	Place	Coach
Skills Practiced	Things to Remember	

Practice Notes

Practice Date	Place	Coach
Skills Practiced	Things to Remember	

Practice Date	Place	Coach
Skills Practiced	Things to Remember	

Practice Notes

Practice Date	Place	Coach
Skills Practiced	Things to Remember	

Practice Date	Place	Coach
Skills Practiced	Things to Remember	

Practice Notes

Practice Date	Place	Coach
Skills Practiced	Things to Remember	

Practice Date	Place	Coach
Skills Practiced	Things to Remember	

Practice Notes

Practice Date	Place	Coach
Skills Practiced	Things to Remember	

Practice Date	Place	Coach
Skills Practiced	Things to Remember	

Practice Notes

Practice Date	Place	Coach
Skills Practiced	**Things to Remember**	

Practice Date	Place	Coach
Skills Practiced	**Things to Remember**	

Practice Notes

Practice Date	Place	Coach
Skills Practiced	**Things to Remember**	

Practice Date	Place	Coach
Skills Practiced	**Things to Remember**	

Practice Notes

Practice Date	Place	Coach
Skills Practiced	**Things to Remember**	

Practice Date	Place	Coach
Skills Practiced	**Things to Remember**	

Goals

Date Goal Set	Target Date to Achieve Goal	Date Goal Achieved
My Goal:	What I Need to Do to Achieve This Goal	

Date Goal Set	Target Date to Achieve Goal	Date Goal Achieved
My Goal:	What I Need to Do to Achieve This Goal	

Date Goal Set	Target Date to Achieve Goal	Date Goal Achieved
My Goal:	What I Need to Do to Achieve This Goal	

Date Goal Set	Target Date to Achieve Goal	Date Goal Achieved
My Goal:	What I Need to Do to Achieve This Goal	

Goals

Date Goal Set	Target Date to Achieve Goal	Date Goal Achieved
My Goal:	What I Need to Do to Achieve This Goal	

Date Goal Set	Target Date to Achieve Goal	Date Goal Achieved
My Goal:	What I Need to Do to Achieve This Goal	

Date Goal Set	Target Date to Achieve Goal	Date Goal Achieved
My Goal:	What I Need to Do to Achieve This Goal	

Date Goal Set	Target Date to Achieve Goal	Date Goal Achieved
My Goal:	What I Need to Do to Achieve This Goal	

Goals

Date Goal Set	Target Date to Achieve Goal	Date Goal Achieved
My Goal:	What I Need to Do to Achieve This Goal	

Date Goal Set	Target Date to Achieve Goal	Date Goal Achieved
My Goal:	What I Need to Do to Achieve This Goal	

Date Goal Set	Target Date to Achieve Goal	Date Goal Achieved
My Goal:	What I Need to Do to Achieve This Goal	

Date Goal Set	Target Date to Achieve Goal	Date Goal Achieved
My Goal:	What I Need to Do to Achieve This Goal	

Goals

Date Goal Set	Target Date to Achieve Goal	Date Goal Achieved
My Goal:	What I Need to Do to Achieve This Goal	

Date Goal Set	Target Date to Achieve Goal	Date Goal Achieved
My Goal:	What I Need to Do to Achieve This Goal	

Date Goal Set	Target Date to Achieve Goal	Date Goal Achieved
My Goal:	What I Need to Do to Achieve This Goal	

Date Goal Set	Target Date to Achieve Goal	Date Goal Achieved
My Goal:	What I Need to Do to Achieve This Goal	

Goals

Date Goal Set	Target Date to Achieve Goal	Date Goal Achieved
My Goal:	What I Need to Do to Achieve This Goal	

Date Goal Set	Target Date to Achieve Goal	Date Goal Achieved
My Goal:	What I Need to Do to Achieve This Goal	

Date Goal Set	Target Date to Achieve Goal	Date Goal Achieved
My Goal:	What I Need to Do to Achieve This Goal	

Date Goal Set	Target Date to Achieve Goal	Date Goal Achieved
My Goal:	What I Need to Do to Achieve This Goal	

Goals

Date Goal Set	Target Date to Achieve Goal	Date Goal Achieved
My Goal:	What I Need to Do to Achieve This Goal	

Date Goal Set	Target Date to Achieve Goal	Date Goal Achieved
My Goal:	What I Need to Do to Achieve This Goal	

Date Goal Set	Target Date to Achieve Goal	Date Goal Achieved
My Goal:	What I Need to Do to Achieve This Goal	

Date Goal Set	Target Date to Achieve Goal	Date Goal Achieved
My Goal:	What I Need to Do to Achieve This Goal	

Goals

Date Goal Set	Target Date to Achieve Goal	Date Goal Achieved
My Goal:	What I Need to Do to Achieve This Goal	

Date Goal Set	Target Date to Achieve Goal	Date Goal Achieved
My Goal:	What I Need to Do to Achieve This Goal	

Date Goal Set	Target Date to Achieve Goal	Date Goal Achieved
My Goal:	What I Need to Do to Achieve This Goal	

Date Goal Set	Target Date to Achieve Goal	Date Goal Achieved
My Goal:	What I Need to Do to Achieve This Goal	

Goals

Date Goal Set	Target Date to Achieve Goal	Date Goal Achieved
My Goal:	What I Need to Do to Achieve This Goal	

Date Goal Set	Target Date to Achieve Goal	Date Goal Achieved
My Goal:	What I Need to Do to Achieve This Goal	

Date Goal Set	Target Date to Achieve Goal	Date Goal Achieved
My Goal:	What I Need to Do to Achieve This Goal	

Date Goal Set	Target Date to Achieve Goal	Date Goal Achieved
My Goal:	What I Need to Do to Achieve This Goal	

Made in United States
Troutdale, OR
11/11/2023

14472066R00046